Sounds & Letters 11

SS

grass	class
glass	dress
chess	kiss
moss	

grass

class

5

glass

dress

9

chess

kiss

moss

grass	class
glass	dress
chess	kiss
moss	

Knowledge Books and Software
PO Box 50 Sandgate, Queensland 4017 Australia
p. +617-55680288 f. +617-55680277 email: sales@kbs.com.au

First Published 2022
ISBN 9781922516831
Text and editing: Carole Crimeen
Design and layout: Suzanne Fletcher
Publisher: Robert Watts

Series Information: **Sounds and Letters**

Credits
Photographs: Cover © Le Manh Thang; p. 1 © FeellFree, Ljupco Smokovski, Pixabay; p. 3 © Dudarev Mikhail; p. 5 © wavebreakmedia; p. 7 © angelo gilardelli; p. 9 © ClickingHappiness; p. 11 © Blaj Gabriel; p. 13 © ideyweb; p. 15 © fongbeerredhot/Shutterstock.

Phonic support books are a wonderful resource for emergent readers as they encourage independent reading and help students make the link between letters and the sounds they represent.

Have students identify the images on the title page to listen for the sound that they will hear through the book.

Encourage students to point to each word as they read through the book.

ISBN: 9781922516831

9 781922 516831 >

KNOWLEDGE BOOKS

Sounds&Letters